THE BRITISH MUSEUM Pocket Timeline of
Ancient Mexico

Penny Bateman

THE BRITISH MUSEUM PRESS

For Paul

© 2009 The Trustees of the British Museum

First published in 2009 by The British Museum Press
A division of The British Museum Company Ltd
38 Russell Square, London WC1B 3QQ

ISBN 978 0 7141 3138 2

Penny Bateman has asserted her right to be identified as
the author of this work.
A catalogue record for this title is available from the
British Library.

Designed by Crayon Design, Brighton
Printed in Malaysia by Tien Wah Press

Mexica / Aztec

The most powerful people in Central Mexico when the Spanish arrived in the sixteenth century were the Mexica. Today they are commonly known as Aztec, and both terms are in use. In this book, the term Mexica is used. (See page 23 for more information.)

Illustration Acknowledgements

Apart from the images listed below, the photographs in this book are copyright the Trustees of the British Museum. Photographs of British Museum objects were taken by Michael Row of the British Museum Photography and Imaging Dept, except for those on page 10 bottom right and page 18 bottom right, which were taken by Leonora Baird-Smith.

The map on page 5 is by Cally Sutherland. (The names shown and the designations used on this map do not imply official endorsement or acceptance by the British Museum.)

© Paul Almasy/CORBIS : Timeline, chacmool from Tula.

The Art Archive/Gianni Dagli Orti: 19.

Penny Bateman 14 top, 15 bottom, 16 bottom, 20 top, 21 top, 22 top, 26 top left.

© Bettmann/CORBIS: 8 top.

© Bodleian Library, University of Oxford. MS. Arch Selden. A.1, fol 60r (Codex Mendoza): 6 bottom left.

© Foundation for the Advancement of Mesoamerican Studies, Inc., www.famsi.org: 22 bottom.

Courtesy of Prof. David Grove: 11 bottom right.

Courtesy of Prof. Joyce Marcus: Timeline, drawing of One Earthquake.

© 2009. Image copyright The Metropolitan Museum of Art/Art Resource/Scala, Florence: 8 bottom.

Colin McEwan: in Timeline: Olmec head.

© Hans Georg Roth/CORBIS: 21 bottom.

Chloë Sayer: 31 top, 31 bottom, plus in Timeline: Market day in Cuetzalan.

Peter Wilson © Dorling Kindersley: 12.

Helen Wolfe 4, 6 top, 6 bottom right, 7 bottom, 13 top, plus in Timeline: Quetzal-Papalotl Palace; Teotihuacan architecture; and Cathedral in Mexico City.

CONTENTS

CENTRAL MEXICO was the home of some of the most important civilizations in the ancient Americas. It is part of a larger region called Mesoamerica, stretching from northern Mexico to what is now El Salvador. For thousand of years before the arrival of Europeans in the sixteenth century, many indigenous groups of people lived in Mesoamerica with their own languages and ways of living. They also shared many common customs and beliefs. From about 2000 BC they farmed. They shared religious beliefs about their world. They were all involved in long distance trade throughout Mesoamerica and beyond. They created societies ruled by elite groups of people. They developed ways of writing, and were skilled in mathematics, astronomy and recording time. They constructed special buildings and plazas (open spaces) for their religious ceremonies.

The Zapotec city of Monte Albán in the Valley of Oaxaca was one of the great centres of Mesoamerican civilization from about 500 BC to AD 800.

The great civilizations of Mesoamerica included the Mexica (commonly known as 'Aztec') in Central Mexico, the Zapotec and later Mixtec in the Valley of Oaxaca, the Totonac on the Gulf Coast of Mexico and the Maya in southern Mexico and northern Central America.

Ancient Mesoamerican peoples showed forces of nature as gods, like this Mexica figure of the goddess of water.

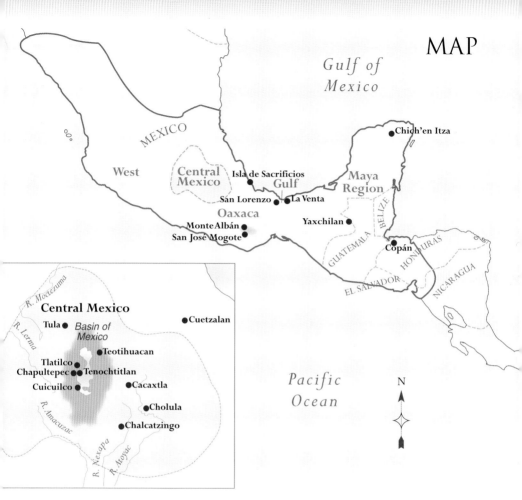

MAP

Gulf of Mexico

MEXICO

West

Central Mexico

Isla de Sacrificios

Gulf

San Lorenzo ● ●La Venta

Oaxaca

Monte Albán ●
San José Mogote ●

Maya Region

Yaxchilan ●

● Chich'en Itza

BELIZE

GUATEMALA

HONDURAS

Copán ●

EL SALVADOR

NICARAGUA

Pacific Ocean

N

Central Mexico

R. Moctezuma

R. Lerma

Tula ●   Basin of Mexico

● Cuetzalan

● Teotihuacan

Tlatilco ●
Chapultepec ●● Tenochtitlan
Cuicuilco ●

● Cacaxtla

R. Amacuzac

● Cholula

● Chalcatzingo

R. Nexapa
R. Atoyac

How to say the sounds of the names

a	= ah	x	= h or sh
e	= ay	j	= h
i	= ee	tl	= tle (as in turtle)
o	= oh	c before a	= k
u	= ew	c before i	= s
hua	= wa		

Examples:

Nahuatl	=	nah **wah** tle
Teotihuacan	=	Tay oh tee **wah** kan
Yaxchilan	=	yash chee **lahn**
Tlatilco	=	Tlah **teel** koh
Tlaloc	=	Tlah lock
Quetzalcoatl	=	Ket-zal-ko-attle

5

ENVIRONMENT AND GEOGRAPHY

The volcano Popacatépetl rises above fertile farm land.

CENTRAL MEXICO is a mountainous region of volcanoes and valleys. In the centre is a plateau, called the Valley or Basin of Mexico. In ancient times, shallow lakes and marshes teemed with birds, animals, fish and insects. The waters provided reeds for crafts and building. People travelled along the waterways by boat. Fertile plains and hills offered excellent farming land. Forests supplied wood and animals for hunting. The mountains were sources of stone and minerals. Plants useful for medicine and clothing grew in the region. There were routes through the mountains. From early on, the people of Central Mexico traded their resources for exotic goods from distant regions.

Mexica man teaching his son to fish.

For thousands of years maguey plants have been used for drink, food, clothing and buildings.

EARLY PEOPLES

In Central Mexico before *c.* 5000 BC nomadic people hunted and gathered plants for food and craft materials. As time passed they began staying near good food supplies for longer periods. People started to tend certain plants. Over thousands of years, many plants cared for by humans became domesticated. That meant the plants could no longer grow without human help. People relied on them for much of their food and

15th-century stone carving of a squash, an important food of Mesoamerica since 7000 BC.

raw materials. The most important domesticated foods in Mesoamerica were maize, beans and squash. Together they provided a very nutritious diet. Other valuable domesticated plants included gourds (used for containers), avocados, chilli peppers and cotton (for cloth). A few species of animals were also domesticated, the main ones being the dog and the turkey. Many of these plants and animals were first domesticated in Mesoamerica, Central and South America.

Bottle gourds were the first domesticated plants known in Mesoamerica.

FIRST CIVILIZATIONS (C. 2000 TO 300 BC)

Farming

97.

A 16th-century Mexica farmer using an age-old method of planting corn.

By ABOUT 1600 BC most people were farmers living in small villages. They still hunted, fished and gathered wild plants. However, most of their time was spent growing their crops, particularly maize. Most farmers relied on rain and the flooding of rivers for water. Some began building canals to channel water to the fields. They built terraced (stepped) fields on the slopes to hold the water on the land. These farming methods and water systems were very successful and farmers were still using them three thousand years later. These methods required more work and more people, but they grew much more food to feed bigger populations.

Villages

Maize shown as a goddess in a 15th-century Mexica sculpture.

As villages became larger, elite groups of people gained more wealth and power. They became powerful by controlling local resources, crafts and religious sites. Some people controlled trade with other areas. High-status people were buried with imported and luxury objects, such as mirrors of iron ore and carved ornaments of shell and jade. Later in this period, villages included public spaces for ceremonies, as well as religious buildings and better houses for the elite. Many villages not only farmed but also produced crafts such as pottery.

The calendar

By 500 BC Mesoamerican people were interested in recording time. The oldest calendar had a cycle of 260 days. It was used for predictions and conducting rituals. Between 400 and 1 BC, Mesoamericans had also begun using another calendar of 365 days based on the cycle of the sun. Different days had different names and symbols.

Children were named after the date of their birth in the 260-day calendar. This 11th-century ruler is called Eight Deer.

Small Central Mexican pottery figurines of women, made around 1500 – 900 BC.

9

Trade and the Olmec

From about 1200 BC, an important culture called Olmec became increasingly powerful, particularly on the Gulf Coast of Mexico. Here people built some of the first Mesoamerican stone monuments, ceremonial places, large public buildings and pyramids. They were also producing fine pottery, carved jade and stone ornaments. Their art showed symbols and images of rulers and religion.

All the cultures of the region, including the towns and villages of Central Mexico, were connected by trade. Olmec art and ideas spread across Mesoamerica along these trade routes. People in each region traded their own resources in exchange for Olmec goods and other luxuries. Major trading items from Central Mexico were incredibly sharp blades made of a natural volcanic glass called obsidian. Central Mexican obsidian was traded to the Olmec centres on the Gulf Coast of Mexico and as far south as the Maya area.

This Olmec ceremonial jade axe has jaguar and caiman features. In Olmec and other Mesoamerican cultures, the colour green symbolized water and the fertility of the earth.

An obsidian core used for striking off blades, and an obsidian flaked point.

Towns

Several Central Mexican villages grew in importance because they controlled local resources or had a good location. The town of Chalcatzingo was situated on a major trade route. Its Olmec-style art showed influences from west Mexico and the Gulf Coast of Mexico. This art included carvings on rock monuments and a nearby cliff face. The extensive religious images showed the essential importance of life-giving water and a fertile earth. Other Central Mexican towns such as Tlatilco also became important because of their foreign trade connections. Fertility figurines of wide-hipped women and seated babies had clear similarities to both West Mexican and Olmec pottery.

The Olmec-influenced carving at Chalcatzingo called *El Rey*, *c.* 900 BC, shows a god or ruler at a cave entrance to the earth, with plants sprouting from its corners.

Olmec-style baby figurine dating to about 1200 – 600 BC.

THE GROWTH OF CITIES (c. 300 to 100 bc)

BETWEEN ABOUT 300 AND 100 BC the population of Central Mexico increased. Some towns grew into cities. Two rival cities in the Basin of Mexico were Cuicuilco in the south and Teotihuacan to the north. But around 150 BC Cuicuilco was partly destroyed by a volcanic eruption and its people moved north to Teotihuacan. Cuicuilco faded in importance and over the next few hundred years Teotihuacan became the major city in Central Mexico.

The pyramid at Cuicuilco.

TEOTIHUACAN (C. 100 BC TO AD 750)

FROM ABOUT 100 BC to AD 450, Teotihuacan grew to be the largest city in the Americas and one of the largest in the world. It eventually had a population of about 130,000 people. At Teotihuacan's heart were two enormous pyramids, as well as ceremonial spaces, palaces and other public buildings. It was the most powerful city in Mesoamerica and was in contact with other major cultures such as the Zapotec in the Valley of Oaxaca and the Totonac on the Gulf Coast of Mexico. It had great influence as far south as the great Maya states in southern Mexico and Guatemala. Some Maya rulers wore Teotihuacan costumes and used Teotihuacan-style art.

One of the two great Teotihuacan pyramids is the enormous Pyramid of the Sun.

A fine carving, c. AD 725, from the Maya city of Yaxchilan, shows the head of a warrior emerging from the mouth of a serpent. The warrior wears a Teotihuacan-style mask of a rain god.

The Pyramid of the Moon was built over hundreds of years. It was finally completed by about AD 400.

A sacred city

The people of Teotihuacan thought the landscape around them was sacred. They built their city so that it was connected to this sacred world. The largest monument, the Pyramid of the Sun, is built over a series of underground cave-like tunnels. In Mesoamerica people believed caves were the entrance to the sacred underworld and the place from where humans first came.

The Pyramid of the Moon was in the shape of the mountain behind it. Two main streets in Teotihuacan stretched out to the four cardinal points, north, south, east and west. Symbolically the city was at the centre of the world.

This Teotihuacan pot is incised with the symbol for 'reptile eye', one of the days in the 260-day ritual calendar.

Religion

Teotihuacan's most important gods represented water, fire and earth, the natural elements critical for human life. One temple was devoted to the Feathered Serpent, Quetzalcoatl. This god was connected to the underworld and the beginning of time. Like many ancient societies in Mesoamerica, people in Teotihuacan believed that their gods required offerings, including human sacrifices. The bodies of sacrificial victims, possibly captured enemies, have been found in the Temple of the Feathered Serpent.

A pot in the form of the god Tlaloc is associated with life-giving rain.

A stone frieze shows the Feathered Serpent and the rain god Tlaloc, both symbols for new beginnings and creation.

Art

This Teotihuacan onyx dish for offerings is in the form of an ocelot. Felines were believed to travel between the natural and spiritual worlds.

Most of Teotihuacan's religious and public buildings were covered in plaster and brightly painted. Many had beautiful murals of animals, mythical creatures, people and gods. These paintings, along with many carved images on sculptures and buildings, provided important information about ruling and religion. People in Teotihuacan used these images to express ideas just as other Mesoamerican people, such as the Maya and Zapotec, used different types of writing systems.

The Teotihuacan wall painting shows a figure, possibly a deity or ruler, as a provider of life-giving resources, such as water.

16

City planning and urban living

The whole city of Teotihuacan was planned on a grid system over drains and canals bringing fresh water to the city. Beyond the main avenues were streets of walled compounds. They enclosed the homes of the people of Teotihuacan.

There were thousands of compounds in the city. Each had numerous rooms, usually surrounding a central patio. This patio provided light, air and a place to collect rainwater. Some of the compounds also had small temples. Related families of between twenty to one hundred people lived in a compound. Families would have rooms for cooking, sleeping, storage and places for garbage. We also know that they buried some of their dead in these compounds. Decorated pots for burning incense and numerous pottery figures, many representing gods, have been found in people's living areas.

These are some of the hundreds of thousands of pottery figurines found in Teotihuacan.

A multicultural cosmopolitan city

Teotihuacan was a huge, bustling city filled with local people and foreigners, merchants and craftspeople. Many neighbourhoods (barrios) were organized by the occupations of the people living there. There were workshops for obsidian tool-making, weaving, pottery, sculpture, feather-work and painting. Different groups of foreigners lived in certain barrios. In one barrio lived people from the Gulf Coast of Mexico. People from Oaxaca lived in another.

Teotihuacan controlled the nearby deposits of clay for pottery, as well as obsidian and other minerals. Its obsidian tools and pottery were exported along the great trade routes all over Mesoamerica. They have been found as far away as Belize in Central America. In return, many foreign goods were imported to the city.

This Maya jade plaque, found in Teotihuacan, was probably imported from the Maya region far to the south.

These human-like figures of obsidian were used as offerings.

AFTER TEOTIHUACAN (c. AD 750 to 900)

By AD 750, Teotihuacan was no longer a great Mesoamerican super-power. What happened? There may have been a food shortage. People may have risen up against the rulers. Other states may have invaded, or destroyed Teotihuacan's trade routes. The city did suffer a great fire. Around AD 650 people began leaving the city and it eventually became a ruin. Centuries later, people travelled to visit this great religious site. The Mexica believed it was built by gods and named it the 'place of the gods' or Teotihuacan.

After the loss of Teotihuacan, Mesoamerica changed. The population of great cities declined. In Central Mexico, smaller cities with strong defences ruled local areas. It was a time of unrest and warfare.

Painted murals in the Central Mexican city of Cacaxtla show battle scenes.

TOLTEC (c. AD 900 to 1200)

The central plaza at Tula was surrounded by pyramids, palaces and public buildings.

THE CULTURE which dominated most of Mesoamerica between AD 900 and 1200 was the Toltec. The later Mexica believed it had been a great civilization of arts and culture. Archaeologists argue whether the Toltec were really a group of people or an art style adopted by many Mesoamerican people. Toltec symbols, art and architecture have been found on the Gulf Coast of Mexico and as far as Central America. The great Maya city of Chich'en Itza shared similar Toltec forms of architecture, sculpture and painting with a smaller city in Central Mexico, called Tula. Tula supported a population of about 30,000 people. Its centre had pyramids and palaces for rituals and for administration. Barrios similar to those in

This Toltec-style pot was used for burning incense. It was found on the Gulf Coast of Mexico at a major Mesoamerican shrine, called Isla de Sacrificios.

This book of the Mixtec people of Oaxaca tells the story of an 11th-century ruler called Eight Deer. Here he greets a representative from the city of Tula.

Teotihuacan were the homes of craftspeople and different ethnic groups. Like other Mesoamerican people of the time, the people of Tula were interested in warfare. On top of Tula's most important pyramid are stone pillars carved in the form of warriors, carrying weapons for hurling spears. They wear chest ornaments shaped like butterflies. Later Mexica people said warriors who died in battle became butterflies. Cities such as Tula fought wars to defend themselves, and also to gain land, luxury goods and sacrificial victims for their religious ceremonies.

The Toltec were the inspiration for the later civilization, the Mexica (who are now often called the Aztec). The Mexica

claimed that their system of government, religion, and art came from the Toltec. Mexica rulers said they were descended from Toltec rulers.

These stone columns at Tula show Toltec warriors.

Tula was abandoned around 1150. People moved to other smaller cities. New groups of people began to settle in Central Mexico.

A Toltec-style sculpture called a chacmool from the Maya city of Chich'en Itza. It was used for religious offerings.

Ball court at Tula.

The ball game

Mesoamericans shared many common customs. One was a ball game played with a solid rubber ball. We don't know the exact rules and they also varied from place to place. Players hit the ball with their padded hips and elbows and maybe bats. A team probably scored by reaching the other team's end or by hitting or passing the ball through a special stone marker. The game was both a spectator sport and a religious event connecting people to the spiritual world. Myths and art describe gods playing the game. The ball in the air may have symbolized the sun in the sky. Ball courts are found in many ancient Mesoamerican cities, including the city of Tula.

A 16th-century drawing showing a Mexica ball game.

MEXICA ('AZTEC') C. AD 1200 TO 1521

MESOAMERICAN LEGENDS tell of a mythical homeland called Aztlan, ruled by leaders called Aztec. A breakaway group called the Mexica were said to have left Aztlan. They migrated to the Basin of Mexico in the thirteenth century and settled there. The Mexica became the most powerful group and the rulers of an empire. (Today they are commonly known as Aztec, but this was not the name they called themselves.) Originally the Mexica worked for other peoples, fighting their wars. Eventually the Mexica founded their own city of Tenochtitlan on an island in a lake. They allied themselves with the nearby cities of Texcoco and Tlacopan. This alliance overthrew the people who were then in power, the Tepanecs, to become the new rulers. Over the years, Mexica rulers created a great empire. It ended, however, when the Spanish under Hernán Cortés arrived in Mexico in 1519. Enemies of the Mexica joined with the Spanish to fight. By 1521, the Mexica empire had been destroyed.

A stone sculpture of the god of dance and feasting, Xochipilli.

The Mexica built their capital where they saw an eagle perched on a cactus. This 16th-century book illustration shows the eagle and cactus.

The city of Tenochtitlan

The capital city of the Mexica was Tenochtitlan. It was the centre of the empire and the largest city. Over 200,000 people lived there. Set on an island in Lake Texcoco, it was an incredible sight, with its white or brightly painted buildings. Long roads or causeways joined the city to the mainland. Huge dykes controlled the lake waters. An aqueduct (man-made channel) brought fresh water from across the salt-water lake. The whole island was criss-crossed by canals filled with canoes transporting goods and people. On the outskirts were small farms. In the city people lived in family compounds of simple houses. Richer homes of noble families were two-storey houses with fine gardens. The city had two great markets and many temples and pyramids. At its heart was the main religious centre as well as the luxurious palaces of the Mexica rulers.

This sculpture, called Xiuhcoatl (Fire Serpent), represents lightning and sun rays. It was originally attached to a building, where it would look as if it were striking earthwards from the sky.

Small pottery temples were used in household shrines.

Gods and religion

Tenochtitlan's sacred centre was filled with many temples. They housed gods connected with nature, planets and stars that the Mexica believed supported them and their rise to power. There were gods of water, fertility and agriculture. Balancing them were gods of the sun, war and death. The main pyramid, the Templo Mayor, was dedicated to the rain god, Tlaloc and to Huitzilopochtli, a god of war and the sun. The Mexica believed this temple was at the centre of the four quarters of the world and between the heavens and the underworld. During its construction, people buried offerings in its foundations, such as shells, pottery and jade from all over the empire.

People believed that their gods had sacrificed themselves to create the earth. In return the gods needed human blood. Without human sacrifice, people believed their world would not survive. Humans, usually war captives, were frequently sacrificed on important religious occasions.

A 16th-century drawing of the Templo Mayor with its twin temples.

This mask represents Tezcatlipoca (Smoking Mirror), a god of rulers and warriors.

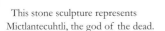
This stone sculpture represents Mictlantecuhtli, the god of the dead.

On the shallow lakes, farmers created fertile raised fields. Some are still farmed today.

These household pottery figures were used in fertility rituals.

Society

The towns and cities of the region were home to over a million people – rulers, priests, administrators and craftsmen, as well as many commoners. The commoners had to pay tribute of labour and goods to the ruling nobles. Nobles helped administer cities and the empire and in return they became wealthy from their lands and from tribute. Nobles paid their own tribute to the rulers of the cities, called *tlatoani*, meaning 'Great Speaker'. The greatest ruler of all was the Mexica *tlatoani* of Tenochtitlan. In 1519 this was Moctezuma II, who ruled 1502–1520.

Many people farmed the land, producing food for the people in the cities. Urban dwellers lived in neighbourhoods with their own temples, community organizations and schools. Girls learnt to cook and weave. Boys learnt the craft of their fathers. Both went to school to learn ritual dancing and songs and boys trained to be warriors. Noble children went to their own schools to learn about religion and governing, and there noble boys were also trained as leaders and warriors.

16th-century drawings of two Mexica commoners.

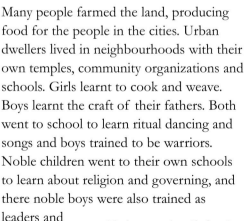

The last great *tlatoani* before the Spanish arrived was Moctezuma II.

Empire

By 1519 the empire covered most of Mesoamerica. As each ruler conquered more city states, increased tribute flowed into Tenochtitlan. The Mexica attacked any city that refused to be under their rule. During battles, Mexica also captured many enemy warriors for sacrifice in religious ceremonies. Experienced warriors led the battles, followed by men wishing to rise in the military ranks by taking captives. The Jaguar and Eagle warriors were two of the highest military orders.

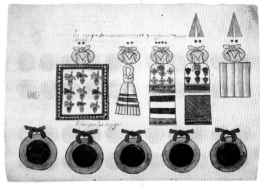

16th-century illustration of tribute, showing obsidian mirrors and fine textiles.

A spear-thrower carved with an image of a warrior.

A defeated state's ruling family was usually kept in power as long as they collected the tribute required by the Mexica. The increased tribute made commoners in the empire poorer, but it made the Mexica ruler and nobles wealthy. It allowed the city's art, architecture and public ceremonies to become increasingly magnificent.

Knife in the form of a warrior dressed as an Eagle knight.

Markets and crafts

The largest of all the markets was the Tlatelolco market in the capital. Over 25,000 people visited it every day. The market sold local foods, raw materials and crafts as well as luxury goods from all over the empire. These included turquoise, jade and other precious stone artefacts, cacao for

Turquoise, one of the most precious materials, came from what is now the southwest United States. This serpent ornament and ritual mask are covered in a mosaic of turquoise.

chocolate (the drink of nobles), finely-woven cotton cloth, brilliant feathers from the southern tropics, red dye made from insects, hard-wearing bronze axes from West Mexico and finely-painted pottery. Judges oversaw the market to prevent cheating or stealing. People bartered and also used cacao beans and cloth as currency.

Luxury goods included fine painted pottery from the city of Cholula.

Most of the sellers were local merchants, craftspeople and farmers. But the foreign, luxury goods were brought by a special group of merchants called the *pochteca*. They travelled the empire and beyond, trading their wares. They lived in their own sections of cities and had their own religious temples and customs.

In almost every home, people were involved in crafts. Women, both nobles and commoners, spun and wove cloth for their families. Most men made tools and weapons. Fine cotton cloth was woven in homes all over the empire as part of the tribute they owed. But there were also specialist craftworkers. Among the most honoured were those who worked with precious stones such as turquoise and jade. Goldsmiths and feather-workers were also highly valued. All made exquisite jewellery, personal ornaments and religious objects. Many of the craftspeople were foreigners who had come to work in Tenochtitlan. Certain towns in the Basin of Mexico also specialized in craft production. The town of Otumba made mould-made pottery, and also tools and fine ornaments of local obsidian.

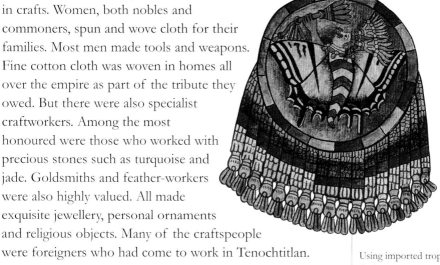

Using imported tropical feathers, specialists created fine feather mosaics such as the shield shown in this 16th-century painting.

A gold ring decorated with a feline face.

A round mirror made of polished obsidian, a type of volcanic glass.

Writing

There had been different forms of writing in Mesoamerica since the sixth century BC. Mexica writing expressed ideas using images and symbols. Mexica scribes wrote books about religion, divining people's fate, the histories of cities and rulers, as well as books recording tribute and other statistics. These books, called codices, were made of deerskin or bark paper folded in a zig-zag. They were beautifully painted by specialist scribes. These men and women were highly honoured for their skill and their knowledge.

A few of these books survived the Spanish conquest. Other books written soon afterwards were also partly written in Mexica style and symbols. They provide us with valuable information about Mexica culture.

This book was written by Mixtec people from Oaxaca. It is similar to Mexica books. This page shows the ruler Eight Deer as an armed warrior, leading an attack.

FROM AD 1519 TO THE PRESENT

IN AD 1521, Spanish rule replaced that of the Mexica state and continued until Mexico became independent in the early nineteenth century.

The Spanish imposed a new system of forced labour and tribute. Epidemics of European diseases reduced the indigenous population by over 80 per cent in the first few decades after the conquest. Most indigenous people were converted to some form of Catholicism. However, language and customs from the earlier time did not disappear and the population eventually revived. Today, over a million people in Central Mexico speak Nahuatl, the language of the Mexica. Many of their traditions are directly descended from those of their ancient ancestors, while others are a fusion of Spanish, Native and world cultures. The name of the country, Mexico, comes from the name of the Mexica people.

This ceramic tree of life, made in 1992 by Mexican artist Tiburcio Soteno Fernandez, shows the encounter between the Mexica and Spanish worlds.

Francisca Rivera Pérez, a speaker of Nahuatl and Spanish from Cuetzalan, Puebla, continues the gauze weaving traditions of her ancestors. She is shown here in 1985 with her mother and children.

FURTHER READING

Art Across the Ages: Ancient Mexico: Level 1, Kelly Campbell Hinshaw, Chronicle, 2007

Aztecs Activity Book, Penny Bateman, British Museum Press, 1994

Aztecs Sticker Book, Susan Raikes, British Museum Press, 2009

Moctezuma and the Aztecs, Elisenda Vila Llonch, British Museum Press 2009

Pocket Dictionary of Aztec and Maya Gods and Goddesses, Clara Bezanilla,
    British Museum Press, 2006

Tenochtitlan, Leonardo López Luján and Judy Levin, Oxford University Press, 2006

Some useful websites:

The British Museum

www.britishmuseum.org

Click on Explore to browse the British Museum's collections online and find online tours and activities. Also, information on Mexica/Aztec buildings and markets can be found on this British Museum site:

www.ancientcivilizations.co.uk

Find out more about the Mesoamerican ball game at:

www.ballgame.org

This website provides resources and activities on Mexico and the Mexica/Aztec:

www.mexicolore.co.uk

Maps and information about ancient Mexico can be found at:

www.ancientweb.org/mexico/

This Time-line tells you about some of the important times, events and people of ancient Central Mexico. Each column covers 300 years of history, except for the first column, which deals with the period before 1200 BC, and the last sections.

For most of this period of time, it is not known exactly when an event happened. In this case, 'c.' appears before the year or period of years. This stands for the Latin word *circa*, which means 'about'.

The dates are numbered backwards and forwards from the year 1, the traditional date for the birth of Jesus Christ. The letters BC stand for 'Before Christ'. AD stands for Anno Domini, 'in the year of our Lord', meaning after the birth of Christ.

Scholars have given special names to different periods in ancient Mesoamerica when new ways of living or new technologies were used. An example is Formative. In the early Formative period, people were farmers and were making pottery. In the Late Formative, the first cities were emerging. In this Time-line the main period names are printed on the colour bar at the top.

■ *c.* 12000 – 5000 BC Nomadic peoples hunt and gather plants for food.

■ *c.* 8000 BC Bottle gourds are the first domesticated plants found in Mexico.

A bottle gourd.

■ *c.* 7000 BC This is the first known date of domesticated squash.

■ *c.* 4000 BC Maize is domesticated in Mexico.

■ *c.* 2000 BC By this time, most people in Central Mexico are farmers.

■ *c.* 1900 – 1750 BC The first pottery in Central Mexico is made.

■ *c.* 1400 – 1350 BC Central Mexican communities produce obsidian tools.

■ *c.* 1300 BC People live in small scattered farming communities, connected by trade.

1201 TO 900 BC

FORMATIVE PERIOD *c.* 1200 BC – 300 BC

■ *c.* 1200 – 1000 BC People of the Central Mexican Tlatilco culture live in large farming villages ruled by chiefs.

■ *c.* 1200 – 900 BC People throughout Mesoamerica begin to trade in luxury goods such as jade, featherwork, shells and pottery, in exchange for local resources such as obsidian.

■ *c.* 1200 – 900 BC The Olmec culture develops along the Gulf Coast of Mexico, particularly at San Lorenzo with its ceremonial centre and stone monuments. Olmec art becomes popular in many parts of Mesoamerica as far as northern Central America.

■ Before *c.* 900 BC Tlatilco people in Central Mexico sometimes bury their dead with Olmec-style pottery figures.

Pottery head from Tlatilco, Valley of Mexico.

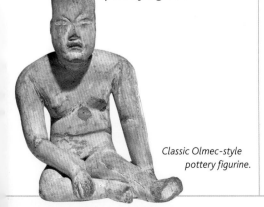

Classic Olmec-style pottery figurine.

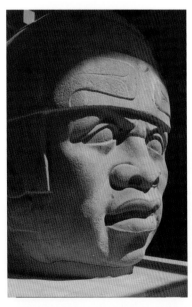

Olmec stone monument portraying a ruler, from San Lorenzo.

Stone carving of a ruler at Chalcatzingo.

■ *c.* 900 BC The interconnection of the Gulf Coast, West and Central Mexico helps to spread Olmec art.

■ *c.* 700 BC The town of Chalcatzingo thrives, partly due to its location on a major trade route with access to local resources such as minerals and cotton.

■ *c.* 600 BC On the Gulf Coast of Mexico, La Venta replaces San Lorenzo as the major Olmec site. Its ceremonial centre with large religious platforms, pyramid and monuments are copied by later Mesoamerican cultures.

■ 600 – 400 BC Olmec jade and greenstone sculptures are important trade items throughout Mesoamerica.

Olmec ceremonial axe carved from jade, probably imported from Guatemala.

■ *c.* 600 – 500 BC Early examples of writing appear in Mesoamerica.

■ *c.* 550 BC The population of the Basin of Mexico rises to about 20,000.

■ *c.* 500 BC By this period, the Mesoamerican 260-day ritual calendar is developed.

■ *c.* 400 BC Olmec monuments at La Venta are damaged. Olmec influence declines.

Pottery figurine of the Chupicuaro style.

■ *c.* 400 – 100 BC Each region begins to develop its own forms of religion and political systems. Olmec art is replaced by other art styles in Central Mexico; for example, the west Mexican Chupicuaro style.

6th-century BC monument at San José Mogote showing a slain person with his name glyph 'One Earthquake' written beside him.

▓ *c.* 300 – 1 BC The population in Central Mexico is increasing and the first cities are emerging.

▓ *c.* 300 BC The small cities of Cuicuilco and Teotihuacan are the major rival centres in the Basin of Mexico.

▓ *c.* 200 BC Cuicuilco becomes the region's major city. It has ceremonial buildings and a massive round pyramid.

▓ *c.* 150 BC Eruption of a volcano buries part of Cuicuilco.

The pyramid at Cuicuilco.

▓ *c.* 100 BC Elsewhere in Mesoamerica new power centres are emerging, such the Maya city of Tikal in Guatemala and the Zapotec city of Monte Albán in Oaxaca.

The initial layout of Monte Albán's main plaza was complete by the 2nd century BC.

C. AD 901 TO 1200

POST CLASSIC PERIOD C. AD 900 – 1521

▓ AD 900 – 1200 The Toltec culture dominates most of Mesoamerica.

▓ c. AD 900 The city of Tula is constructed.

▓ c. AD 900 – 1200 The city of Tula trades with the Gulf Coast of Mexico, Oaxaca and even has connections with Costa Rica.

▓ c. AD 900 – 1200 There are strong Toltec influences at the Maya city of Chich'en Itza, as shown in its art and architecture.

▓ AD 998 A Toltec-style carving at the Maya city of Chich'en Itza has a date of AD 998.

A Toltec-style chacmool from Chich'en Itza.

Remains of the city of Tula.

Stone figure, called a chacmool, from a building at Tula. A hollow cavity on the figure's stomach was used for offerings.

16th-century drawing of the Mexica's homeland, Aztlan. Aztlan gave rise to the name 'Aztec'.

■ *c.* AD **1200** People called the Mexica arrive in Central Mexico from their legendary homeland of Aztlan. Today they are often called Aztec, but that is not the name they called themselves.

16th-century drawings describing a Mexica defeat by the Culhua ruler at Chapultepec (Grasshopper Hill) and, below, Mexica fleeing on rafts.

■ *c.* AD **1200 – 1300** City-states dominate Central Mexico.

■ AD **1250 – 1325** Mexica are mercenaries of the city of Culhua until they kill a Culhua princess and are forced to flee.

■ AD **1325** Mexica found the city of Tenochtitlan on an island in Lake Texcoco.

■ AD **1428** An alliance of the Mexica, Texcoco and Tlacopan people defeat the Tepanecs and establish an empire.

■ AD **1458** The ruler Moctezuma I expands the Mexica empire to the Gulf Coast and Oaxaca.

Fragment of a stone box with the symbol for Ahuizotl, the name of a Mexica ruler.

16th-century drawing showing the death of Ahuizotl and Moctezuma II as the new ruler.

■ AD 1486 – 1502 The Mexica ruler Ahuizotl expands the empire with major trade routes as far as western Guatemala.

■ AD 1502 – 1519 Moctezuma II strengthens control of the Mexica empire.

A spear-thrower carved with the figure of a Mexica warrior.

■ AD 1519 The Spanish, led by Hernán Cortés, come face to face with the Mexica under their ruler, Moctezuma II.

■ AD 1520-1 The first epidemic of European diseases kills hundreds of thousands of indigenous people.

■ AD 1520 Moctezuma II is killed, replaced by Cuitlahuac and then Cuauhtemoc, the last Mexica ruler.

■ AD 1521 700 Spanish soldiers and 70,000 allies defeat the Mexica and their allies.

■ AD 1522 Mexica public buildings, temples and books are destroyed.

Image of a Spanish ship off the coast of Mexico, from an early 16th-century book.

An 8th-century Maya stone carving showing a warrior emerging from the mouth of a snake. He is wearing a Teotihuacan-style rain god mask.

■ *c.* AD 600 – 750 Teotihuacan declines in power.

■ *c.* AD 600 Central Mexican cities, such as Cacaxtla, have more defences and are more involved in warfare.

■ *c.* AD 700 – 800 Many of Teotihuacan's buildings are burnt and most of the population leaves.

■ AD 725 Maya rulers at the city of Yaxchilan still use Teotihuacan art as propaganda to support their right to rule.

■ *c.* AD 800 – 900 Small bands of people live in Teotihuacan while new groups of people come from the north and east to settle in Central Mexico.

■ *c.* AD 850 As some Maya cities decline in power, new Maya cities in the Yucatán become important, such as Chich'en Itza.

Paintings at Cacaxtla showing battle scenes.

■ *c.* AD 300 – 600 The city of Teotihuacan is at its largest.

■ *c.* AD 300 – 450 Teotihuacan has powerful influence throughout Mesoamerica as far as southern Maya cities.

■ AD 426 – 487 K'inich Yax K'uk' Mo', founder of the Maya city of Copan, is supported in his rule by Teotihuacan.

8th-century portrait of the 5th-century Copan ruler K'inich Yax k'uk' Mo' with Teotihuacan-style 'goggles'.

■ *c.* AD 400 The final stage of Teotihuacan's Pyramid of the Moon is completed.

■ *c.* AD 400 – 500 Goods and people flow into Teotihuacan from other regions.

■ *c.* AD 450 Teotihuacan craft production is at its highest with mass produced mould-made figurines.

Teotihuacan mould-made pottery figurines.

Jade plaque found at Teotihuacan, imported from the Maya area.

▨ *c.* AD 1 By now, Teotihuacan is the major city in Central Mexico. Over the next few hundred years it grows into the largest city in Mesoamerica.

▨ *c.* AD 100 The first major construction of Teotihuacan's Pyramid of the Moon begins.

▨ *c.* AD 100 –150 The Pyramid of the Sun in Teotihuacan is built.

▨ *c.* AD 150 – 300 New palaces and public buildings are constructed as Teotihuacan's population grows.

▨ *c.* AD 150 – 300 The building complex with the Temple of the Feathered Serpent is constructed.

▨ *c.* AD 200 – 350 Apartment compounds are built throughout Teotihuacan along with the city's water and drainage system.

The Pyramid of the Moon at Teotihuacan.

Typical Teotihuacan architecture with slanted stepped walls called talud-tablero.

Teotihuacan's Palace of Quetzal-Papalotl.